I0796113

AMERICAN HEROES

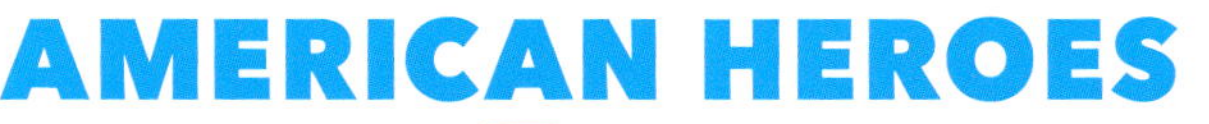

ZITKÁLA-ŠÁ
NATIVE WRITER AND ACTIVIST

by Becca Becker

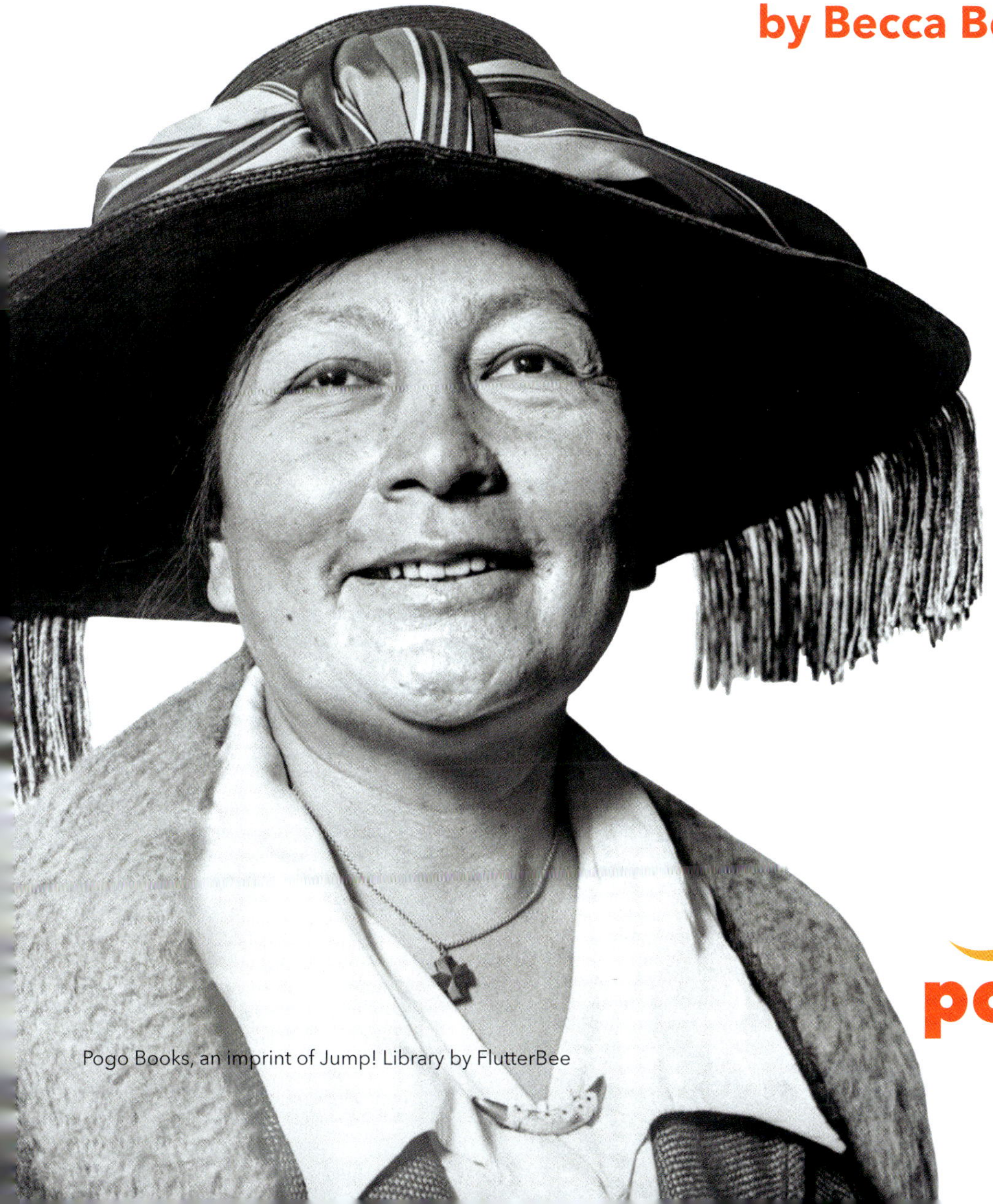

pogo

Pogo Books, an imprint of Jump! Library by FlutterBee

Ideas for Parents and Teachers

Pogo Books let children practice reading informational text while introducing them to nonfiction features such as headings, labels, sidebars, maps, and diagrams, as well as a table of contents, glossary, and index.

Carefully leveled text with a strong photo match offers early fluent readers the support they need to succeed.

Before Reading

- "Walk" through the book and point out the various nonfiction features. Ask the student what purpose each feature serves.
- Look at the glossary together. Read and discuss the words.

During Reading

- Have the child read the book independently.
- Invite them to list questions that arise from reading.

After Reading

- Discuss the child's questions. Talk about how they might find answers to those questions.
- Prompt the child to think more. Ask: Zitkála-Šá spoke up about her beliefs. What can you do to speak up for what you believe?

Pogo Books are published by Jump!
3500 American Blvd W, Suite 150
Bloomington, MN 55431
www.jumplibrary.com

Jump! is a division of FlutterBee Education Group.

Library of Congress Cataloging-in-Publication Data

Names: Becker, Becca, author
Title: Zitkála-Šá: native writer and activist / by Becca Becker.
Description: Bloomington, MN: Jump!, Inc., [2026]
Series: American heroes | Includes index.
Audience: Ages 7-10
Identifiers: LCCN 2025035267 (print)
LCCN 2025035268 (ebook)
ISBN 9798896623700 hardcover
ISBN 9798896623717 paperback
ISBN 9798896623724 ebook
Subjects: LCSH: Zitkala-S̆a, 1876-1938—Juvenile literature.
Yanktonai Indians—Biography—Juvenile literature.
Indian authors—Biography—Juvenile literature.
Indian women activists—Biography—Juvenile literature.
Classification: LCC E99.Y26 B43 2026 (print)
LCC E99.Y26 (ebook)
LC record available at https://lccn.loc.gov/2025035267
LC ebook record available at https://lccn.loc.gov/2025035268

Editor: Katie Chanez
Designer: Molly Ballanger

Photo Credits: Bettmann/Getty, cover, 1, 20-21; goldpix/Adobe Stock, 3; Gertrude Käsebier/Wikimedia, 4, 10; Library of Congress, 5, 8-9, 14-15, 17, 18-19; Pierre Jean Durieu/Shutterstock, 5 (inset); Universal History Archive/Getty, 6-7; Amherst College Collection of Native American Literature, 11 (foreground); Andrea Izzotti/Adobe Stock, 11 (background); IanDagnall Computing/Alamy, 12-13; Ivan Dmitri/Michael Ochs Archives/Getty, 14; Internet Archive, 16; U.S. Mint, 23.

Printed in the United States of America at Corporate Graphics in North Mankato, Minnesota.

TABLE OF CONTENTS

CHAPTER 1

EARLY LIFE

Zitkála-Šá was born on February 22, 1876. She was an American Indian. She was part of the Yankton Dakota Sioux Tribe. She lived on the Yankton Indian **Reservation**. This is in South Dakota.

Native people have lived in North America for thousands of years. The Yankton once traveled across the **Great Plains**. They hunted bison. They lived in **tepees**. Native people still have rich **cultures** today.

In the early 1800s, the Yankton had millions of acres of land. But white people took almost all of it. The U.S. government forced all Native people to live on small reservations.

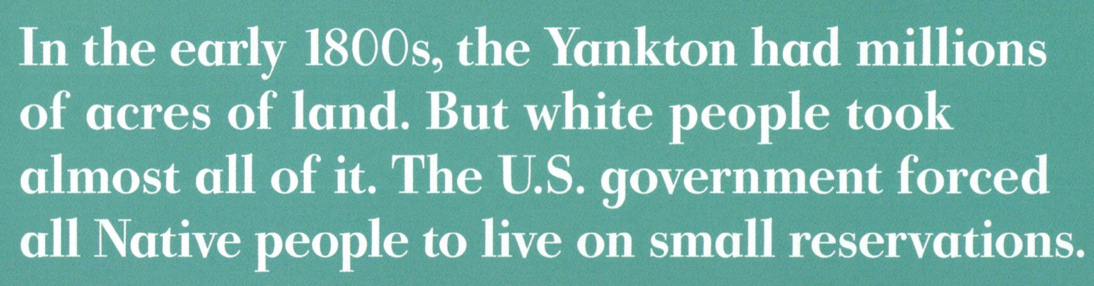

reservation

TAKE A LOOK

What land did American Indians have before the U.S. government took it? What land belongs to them today? Take a look.

American Indian boarding school

The U.S. government took Native children. It put them in **boarding schools**. Why? It wanted to teach them how to act like white people.

In 1884, Zitkála-Šá was eight years old. She was put in a boarding school in Indiana. The school didn't let her speak her Native language. Teachers hurt her if she didn't speak English. They didn't like her long hair. Why? It was part of her culture. They cut it off. Zitkála-Šá cried.

WHAT DO YOU THINK?

The U.S. government didn't want Native people to speak their own languages. It didn't want them to practice their beliefs. How would you feel if your way of life was taken away from you?

CHAPTER 2

WRITING AND MUSIC

Zitkála-Šá finished school in 1895. She went to a music school in Boston, Massachusetts. She played the violin. She was very good!

Zitkála-Šá learned more about Native cultures. She talked to other Native people. She wrote down their histories and stories. She made them into a book. Its title is *Old Indian Legends*.

In 1900, Zitkála-Šá started writing about how unfairly Native people were treated. Her writings were powerful. They were in magazines.

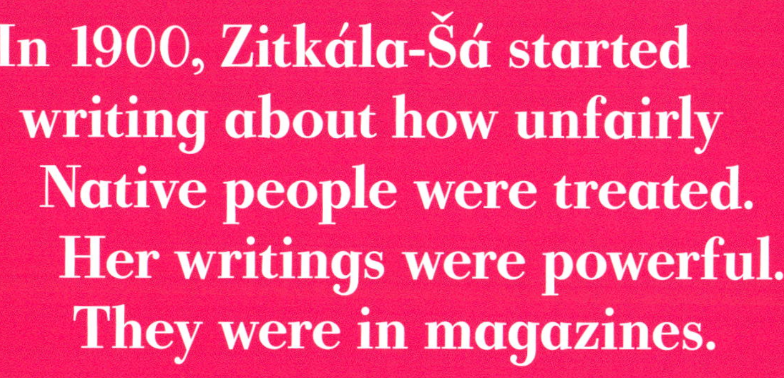

In 1902, she married Raymond Bonnin. He was Yankton Sioux, too. They moved to Utah. They lived on the Uintah and Ouray Reservation. They had a baby boy.

DID YOU KNOW?

Some people were mad about Zitkála-Šá's writings. Others thought she was brave for speaking out.

Zitkála-Šá also wrote music. Between 1910 and 1913, she helped write the first American Indian **opera**. It was called *Sun Dance Opera*.

The Sun Dance is a Native dance. The U.S. government said Native people couldn't do it anymore. But Zitkála-Šá put it in her opera. She helped write the music. She made sure the dances and costumes were right.

Sun Dance

4 THE FARMER AND MECHANIC.

OPERA on the INDIAN RESERVATION in UTAH

CHORUS "THE SUN DANCE OPERA"

"OLD SIOUX": A 90 YEAR OLD PERFORMER COUSIN OF SITTING BULL

COPYRIGHT WM. F. HANSON 1913

"ZITKA SA" AND WILLIAM F HANSON COMPOSERS OF THE SUN DANCE

TAR HEELS NOT AFTER POSTAL SAVINGS BONDS

Indian Girl Writes Opera.

AT last there has been produced an indisputably American opera, "The Sun Dance," written by Zitkala Sa, a full blooded Sioux Indian, the wife of Mr. R. T. Bonnin, an employe of the government on the Uintah Indian Reservation at Vernal, Utah, collaborating with Professor W. Hansen.

The opera, which was recently given at the academy on the reservation, tells the story of the return of the sun from its death during the winter, of the kindliness of its light and warmth as it falls on the earth, of the plants and the trees that spring forth and grow under its rays, and of the whole world rejoic-

Mrs. R. T. Bonnin (Zitkala Sa).

CHAPTER 3

FIGHTING FOR RIGHTS

Zitkála-Šá was not a U.S. **citizen**. Not many Native people were. Why? The U.S. government wanted them to act like white people. Then they could become citizens. Native people didn't have the same **rights** as U.S. citizens. They could not vote for people who would help them.

In 1916, Zitkála-Šá moved to Washington, D.C. She fought for Native people's rights. She wrote for a magazine. She helped show why American Indians should be U.S. citizens.

Washington, D.C., 1918

She was an **activist**. She spoke across the country. She asked people to save Native cultures. She even spoke to **Congress**. She told them how Native people's rights were being ignored.

Congress listened to her. In 1924, Congress passed the Indian Citizenship Act. Calvin Coolidge was president. He signed it into law. The act said American Indians were U.S. citizens.

WHAT DO YOU THINK?

Not all American Indians wanted to be U.S. citizens. They did not want to give up their ways of life. How do you think this felt?

Calvin Coolidge

Zitkála-Šá talked to Native people. She told them why it was important to vote. They could make their communities better! But some states made them pass hard reading tests. They made them pay money to vote. This was unfair. Zitkála-Šá kept working. She fought for Native rights until 1938. She passed away that year. Her work will always be remembered.

QUICK FACTS & TOOLS

TIMELINE

What are big events in Zitkála-Šá's life? Take a look!

FEBRUARY 22, 1876
Zitkála-Šá is born on the Yankton Indian Reservation.

1884
Zitkála-Šá goes to a boarding school in Indiana.

1895
Zitkála-Šá finishes school.

1900
Zitkála-Šá begins writing about how Native people are treated.

1901
Zitkála-Šá publishes her book *Old Indian Legends*.

1902
Zitkála-Šá marries Raymond Bonnin.

1910–1913
Zitkála-Šá helps make the first American Indian opera, *Sun Dance Opera*.

1916
Zitkála-Šá moves to Washington, D.C. She works for change.

JUNE 2, 1924
President Calvin Coolidge signs the Indian Citizenship Act.

1926
Zitkála-Šá starts traveling the country. She tells Native people to vote.

JANUARY 26, 1938
Zitkála-Šá passes away at 61 years old.

GLOSSARY

activist: A person who supports a cause and believes in taking action to change things.

boarding schools: Schools that students live in.

citizen: A person who belongs to a country and has full rights.

Congress: The part of the U.S. government that makes laws.

cultures: Ideas, customs, traditions, and ways of life of groups of people.

Great Plains: A large area of grasslands that stretches from Canada to Texas.

Native: A member of the first people who lived in North America.

opera: A play in which all or most of the words are sung and there is an orchestra that plays music.

reservation: An area of land American Indians were allowed to keep and that some still live on today.

rights: Things you are allowed to do.

tepees: Cone-shaped tents that American Indians of the Great Plains used.

INDEX

TO LEARN MORE

Finding more information is as easy as 1, 2, 3.

1. **Go to www.factsurfer.com**
2. **Enter "Zitkala-Sa" into the search box.**
3. **Choose your book to see a list of websites.**